THE
WILSON
READING
SYSTEM

STUDENT
READER
FIVE

by Barbara A. Wilson

SECOND EDITION

Wilson Language Training
162 West Main Street
Millbury, Massachusetts 01527-1943
(508) 865-5699

ISBN 1-56778-016-4 8.00 Student Reader Five   Item# SR5

ISBN 1-56778-010-5 33.00 Student Readers 1-6   Item# WRS116

ISBN 1-56778-009-1 78.00 Student Readers 1-12   Item# WRS112

ISBN 1-56778-000-8 196.00 WRS Complete Set   Item# WRS101

The Wilson Reading System is published by:

Wilson Language Training
162 West Main Street
Millbury, MA 01527-1943

Printed in the U.S.A.

S T E P

5

Concepts

cry	flu	ho
pro	hi	sky
ply	be	so
shy	spry	me
we	fry	by

no	sly	try
ye	go	my
fly	I	he
sty	pi	she
lo	pry	thy

tro	plu	re
che	fi	clo
sple	sle	cha
ky	bri	spo
bro	de	gri

---

ste	sha	plo
spu	twy	cle
dro	spro	tro
bre	stru	de
lu	chi	mo

---

fi	sle	mo
shra	dra	ri
plu	po	thry
thu	fla	re
cly	bli	po

---

za	stry	je
bu	e	spru
sle	scra	cre
fru	gri	o
tha	spro	u

---

ne	blid	thren
pute	bli	threne
shipe	blipe	plo
cho	pru	stome
chot	spone	cret

---

plit	ste	slabe
bri	tome	gly
grome	quo	glip
mupe	shene	chi
gam	bla	scret

---

1. I think that he is shy with Kate.

2. I wish that Tom would be less impulsive.

3. My husband is a golf pro at that club.

4. If Ed gets a bass in this lake, then I will try to fry it.

5. My Gram went to Wisconsin with us, but she did not like to fly.

6. Dave had the flu; Jill spent time with him and she ended up with it.

7. Jake felt as if he would cry when he lost so much cash on his bad investment.

8. I think that the salesman was quite sly.

9. We expect to get this mess up by the time Mom gets home.

10. We must take steps now so that the impact will not be so bad.

Second

The Sly Plan

James did not want to go to school. He was in the second grade. He did like school, but at times, he just did not wish to go. James had a sly plan. He told his mom that he had the flu.

Mom said, "My,my! Good try James, but you must go. You are an old pro with the flu trick, but I think you are well." By the time he was set for school, the bus had left. His mom had to drive him to school, then fly to get to her job on time.

bronco	decode	begin
hotel	recline	protest
resale	silent	relate
prolong	mucus	program
event	canine	demand

---

ditto	divest	focus
eject	behave	yo-yo
tulip	student	stucco
native	propel	repent
stipend	spoken	solo

---

skyline	unite	lilac
motel	profane	prevent
pupil	menu	Cupid
cubic	revere	crisis
retire	feline	hello

---

require	migrate	revive
biplane	deprive	remote
banjo	rodent	veto
locate	frozen	moment
profile	broken	ozone

---

remote	decal	repel
robot	secret	sequel
omit	began	lotus
basic	basin	raven
deduct	reject	climax

---

minus	bisect	siren
moment	rodent	item
depend	respect	trisect
Polish	tripod	basis
polite	request	defect

---

beware	elope	prepare
female	define	deprive
denote	vacate	spoken
tempo	detach	erect
erase	devote	stipend

---

erupt	hatred	halo
declare	mutate	sinus
revise	rebate	open
provide	predict	rotate
silo	unit	vibrate

---

respond	potent	humid
protect	proton	repress
rabbi	minus	rerun
dilate	equate	detest
hifi	even	haven

---

dilute	donate	stupid
zenith	duplex	edict
rebel	refresh	siren
profess	lotto	totem
deplete	stucco	gusto

---

jello	frequent	ditto
debate	bisect	restrict
tempo	bonus	apex
elate	limbo	defrost
deflect	refine	pre-shrunk

---

regret	relent	promote
bingo	Dacron	despite
refund	relax	revoke
result	depict	defend
decline	defect	motto

<u>cri</u>mope	<u>re</u>strimp	<u>g</u>lestome
<u>pre</u>stope	<u>try</u>mest	<u>tru</u>mepe
<u>cl</u>emost	<u>fl</u>oment	<u>pl</u>oshent
<u>stre</u>blent	<u>plo</u>ton	<u>fro</u>lipe
<u>g</u>losop	<u>tre</u>nete	<u>pre</u>spere

<u>bry</u>tome	<u>cro</u>zump	<u>bl</u>enet
<u>r</u>ebelt	<u>d</u>emest	<u>pro</u>trum
<u>b</u>enap	<u>tri</u>glone	<u>tri</u>dem
<u>fl</u>othine	<u>gry</u>stod	<u>sto</u>mest
<u>d</u>elum	<u>re</u>flimp	<u>gli</u>mote

---

1. The student could not relax until the test was complete.

2. Tom did regret that he made the spill on the rug.

3. Jim had a decal on his pink van.

4. The men will prepare to go on strike.

5. You must protect your skin in the sun.

6. It will depend on the last program.

7. Let's relax in the basement by the fire.

8. Tom was quite polite when he spoke.

9. We must request a refund on this dress.

10. Jim will be silent when he gets the best athlete prize.

1. He must deduct that item from the bill.

2. We will check-in at the hotel and then go dine.

3. Jim cannot prevent the dispute at the shop.

4. I wish we could escape from this humid day.

5. Bob will donate cash to the Crisis Fund.

6. Tim will deflate the raft and store it in the shed.

7. We must not disrupt the big event.

8. Jim and Bev Fresco had a big duplex in Boston.

9. A student in my class is in Poland on a trip.

10. I will relax at the lake with Bob and Tom.

1. We hope to prevent any problems with this contract.

2. I regret that I cannot make the event.

3. Bill will have to defend his request.

4. My dad went to the shop to demand a refund.

5. We will spend some time at that motel.

6. I admit that I like this program.

7. The lake is frozen so we can skate.

8. We cannot locate the new dentist.

9. I predict that they will elect Mr. Smith.

10. Did the student behave while I was out?

1. The staff can provide the help you need.

2. I cannot depend on Brad if it is a hot, humid day.

3. Bill plans to retire to devote time to the project.

4. I hope that cat can take care of the rodent.

5. Bob has a secret to tell Fran.

6. The class was silent when Mr. Smith came in.

7. I regret that last vote.

8. Can you donate to this program?

9. My boss is a female on the go.

10. I will escape to the hotel.

1. Did Tom deflate the raft and store it in the shed ?

2. We have to repel these insects !

3. In a moment, I will tell you that joke.

4. The men and women will prepare to go on strike.

5. I would like to inquire about the crisis.

6. I demand that you locate the boy.

7. His hatred made him a very sad man.

8. We will get some tulips in April.

9. That stone chapel is a sacred shrine.

10. A dog is a canine; a cat is a feline.

5.2

1. At the very last moment, Tom sunk the basket to win the game.

2. This student is quite polite in class.

3. The mob will yell in protest.

4. Would you like to begin the objective test?

5. We have a pupil from Hopedale in this class.

6. The Irish Pub is lots of fun.

7. Bill did declare that the lake was o.k. for swimming.

8. It is human to make a mistake.

9. We must repent for our sins.

10. Jim told Beth that he did like her fragrant smell.

1. I hope that they do not destruct the old mill.

2. The cop must direct traffic on Brazen St.

3. We will depend on Jim to make up a motto for our club.

4. Dr. Jones will prescribe a pill for my flu.

5. Eject that tape and put in this one.

6. Tom did request that she open the gift.

7. Mr. Jones will protest the strike.

8. Jim likes to pretend that he is rich, but he is quite broke!

9. Rewind the film so we can see it again.

10. We must restrict the time that you spend under the sunlamp.

1. Bob did not respond to my note.

2. The kids hid in the silo and had lots of fun.

3. I must insist that you complete that task this moment.

4. He did not tell me to wipe the tripod.

5. You must declare the profit and file the tax form.

6. I must omit the badminton game so that I will have time for tennis.

7. Babs and Ed plan to go to that remote ranch and relax!

8. I think that this is a defect in the silk.

9. James makes frequent trips to Manhattan.

10. Kate will get that expensive item despite Tom's protest.

The Basement Mess

Mike had to ask his mom if he could go to the game.

"That depends on your dad," she said, "He will be home at six. He told me that he had plans for you to help him in the basement."

When Mike's dad came home, Mike was quick to ask him about the game. His dad said, "Mike, the game will be lots of fun, but you made the mess in the basement. You can go to the game the moment you finish with me. I insist that you complete the task."

Mike was upset. He would miss lots of the game. He had to admit that his dad did provide some help. At last, the task was complete. Dad said that the basement was fine. Mike ran off to the game and had fun.

5.2

The Bingo Game

Kate and Mrs. Migrane went to the bingo game. The tempo of the game was quite fast. They did not relax at all! They had to focus on the call so that they did not miss a thing. The entire hall was silent. Kate just had to get a "B-nine". She did prepare to yell bingo.

As the moments went by, she could feel the climax. This was the biggest game of all. Then the call came - "B-nine." <u>BINGO!</u> Kate collected the five-hundred dollar prize! Not bad for a night of fun.

The Project

Tom and Beth must devote lots of time to that project. The boss had given them a profile that did describe what they had to do. It was quite complex, and they did wish to accomplish it without lots of help. They did not relax at all.

Tom and Beth did plan to do the best job on it and not stop for a moment. In five days the entire project was complete. The boss did not expect it then. He felt that the result must not be what he had wanted. Then Tom and Beth had to present the project to him. The boss had to admit that it did fill his request. It was well done! Beth and Tom were glad.

5.2

The Stucco Home

Jane went for a long drive. She was lost, but she did not care. She went down a small street. At the end, there was an old stucco home for sale. Jane got out to inspect it. It was such a tranquil spot! The dwelling sat at the top of a hill with stone steps up to it. She felt like this home had been made for her!

That night, Jane told her husband, Rob, about the stucco home. He felt he could predict the cost - expensive! Still, he said that he would inquire about it with her. He did like the prospect as well.

Jane made the call to the salesman. They set up a time to go see the home. Jane and Rob went but did not dare to hope. When they drove down the street, Rob felt the same as Jane: he did like the remote spot. Inside the home, Jane and Rob were in a daze.

The home had felt neglect, but Rob and Jane could revive it. They could expect problems from an old home like this. At last Rob did inquire about the cost. On the basis that it would require lots of work to update it, the cost was not bad. It was inexpensive for the size of the home and land.

Rob and Jane were ecstatic! Most of the time they were not impulsive, but this time, they felt that the stucco home that sat on the hill was just for them.

The Jake Debate

The students in Mrs. Russel's debate class had to prepare for the congressmen's visit. They had to profile each congressman.

Jake had to respect the congressmen and be silent while they had their debate. Jake was not the best kid in the class, but he did behave at the event. He wanted to yell protests, but he was not rude and did repress his comments. Despite all this, Jake did find that the class was quite good. At the end of the debate, the kids had time to dispute the congressmen in a polite way. Jake did this well. Mrs. Russel went up to Jake and said, "You did so well! I think that you can now have a dispute and still respect the other person. You get an <u>A</u> for the day!"

jelly	brandy	jetty
lobby	belly	buggy
lady	jolly	Jimmy
plenty	happy	fifty
silly	handy	ruby

---

baby	penny	daddy
empty	granny	nasty
holy	dandy	trolly
nifty	sunny	petty
caddy	Molly	sulky

---

duty	sultry	angry
dolly	crazy	Tammy
candy	hilly	sentry
pony	lumpy	navy
pantry	copy	holy

tidy	sixty	ivy
taffy	puny	grumpy
gravy	lazy	filthy
tiny	bunny	lady
Betsy	sissy	daffy

Sandy	funny	crony
dizzy	bumpy	Timmy
envy	flashy	Tony
mammy	puppy	shinny
cozy	silky	skinny

sloppy	crunchy	kinky
ditty	lanky	crusty
canny	Lenny	granny
Toby	hilly	prissy
Henry	zany	slinky

1. Jim's instinct told him not to trust the lady in his store.

2. The congressmen will debate in the lobby of the hotel.

3. Did Molly get the expensive ruby from Tim?

4. I dislike this lumpy gravy.

5. Dad will take Sandy to the ranch for a pony ride.

6. That old man is so, so jolly!

7. The entire cabin was so filthy the kids had to spend the day with dust cloths and mops.

8. It has been so humid in the Midwest lately.

9. Betty is such a silly kid.

10. Dad demands that I empty this trash can at this moment, before I go to the game.

1. The press felt it was their duty to publish all the facts in this case.

2. The baby got a tan on her belly.

3. Mom was selfish with the candy, so she hid it on the top shelf.

4. Mr. Jones had to depend on his staff, so he got quite angry if they did not do the job.

5. Get the chestnuts in the pantry.

6. I think that Sally made a nasty comment to Jane.

7. Jim must provide us with a copy of his plans.

8. Let's ride the trolly to the shopping malls.

9. The student has plenty of talent in that subject.

10. Mr. Smith is sixty-five and still has lots of spunk so he did not wish to retire at all.

1. James is quite handy at the shop.

2. Jenny will smile if her daddy brings her home a puppy.

3. The moment Jane left, Jim felt lonely.

4. Tommy had plenty of cash to bring to the big event.

5. Mom had to prepare Molly so that she would be polite when she went to visit.

6. I can detect the smell of brandy.

7. At times, that crazy kid does not behave.

8. Jimmy will try the navy, and his dad hopes that he will like it.

9. Molly made this commitment, but she is lazy and has not done it yet.

10. Did Sally protest at all when she went to get her flu shot?

1. I think that Mr. Kilty is happy with this effective plan.

2. Mom likes to get lots of holly for our home.

3. Jimmy dislikes jelly in his donut.

4. James intends to close up the shop and tidy it before he goes home.

5. The boss expects this job to be complete in plenty of time.

6. The baby was so tiny when she came home.

7. Bob and Jane like to collect nifty things.

8. Sandy's ivy plant will do well in that spot.

9. The bishop went to discuss the holy tablet.

10. Jenny is not a sissy; she is just a lady.

The Pony Ride

Betsy was five years old. She had a life-long wish to go on a pony ride. She had made this request many times. At last, her daddy came home and said, "Betsy, let's go on that pony ride."

Dad, Mom, and Betsy went for a long drive to a big ranch. Then they went to see the pony. Betsy did not run up to it. She hid behind her dad and acted shy. It did take her some time to behave bravely.

At last, Betsy got on the pony. A puppy ran with the pony and Betsy had fun. On the way home, Mom said, "Let's stop to get a milkshake!"

Betsy felt it was the all-time best day of her life!

5.3

Room at the Ritz

A lady went into the lobby of the expensive Ritz Hotel. She went up to the desk and began to demand the best room in the hotel. The man behind the desk did try to be polite, but she did not let him respond. She became angry because the best room had been taken. She said that the room was hers and that the hotel had made a mistake. The lady became quite nasty.

Her protest made the man upset, but he did not yell. At last, he got the lady a room. It was not the best one, but she had to take it.

The Jolly Menu

Sandy had a long day. She went home with a plan to fix a ham. When she got home, the ham was still frozen! She did not defrost it and now she did not have time. The menu was useless without the ham.

She went into the pantry. She had plenty of meat left from the night before. Sandy did not wish to have the same thing, so she made a gravy to go with it.

When her husband, Ted, came home, he was set to dine. The menu was not the best; the gravy was so lumpy! Ted was jolly and made jokes to console Sandy. She did not find it funny. Sandy felt it was a shame not to have the ham.

Henry will Retire

Henry was set to retire at sixty-five. At last, he could begin to relax. He did not mind at all. Henry had a tiny shop in his basement. He was a self-made man, quite handy with welding.

Henry had done plenty of work his entire life. He was glad to say farewell to it. He intended to recline the moment he sold his shop.

The shop was sold and now he could spend his life-long savings. Henry had done his duty; now he would fly south to an expensive hotel and take a long, long sunbath at last!

violate	demolish	develop
absolute	requirement	hydroplane
rejuvenate	despondent	equipment
obsolete	coconut	electron
delinquent	graduate	elastic

---

detachment	demonic	communize
espresso	refreshment	regulate
isolate	microscope	humankind
stipulate	communist	cohesive
disrespect	democratic	invasive

---

evaluate	destructive	development
microscopic	romantic	opponent
represent	remodel	immunize
impolite	responsive	repulsive
economy	patronize	enemy

evacuate	diagnosis	congregate
colonist	economize	explosive
diplomat	defensive	educate
hemoglobin	electrode	retrospect
insulin	itemize	tabulate

novelty	stimulate	majesty
volcano	video	suffocate
tuxedo	faculty	soft-spoken
re-collect	incubate	defiant
violin	egotist	dioxide

---

stipulate	strangulate	succulent
utensil	monopolize	open-minded
humanistic	humanize	monotone
re-enlist	protective	reflective
patronize	amputate	accumulate

---

1.   Mr. Griffin must not violate his contract.

2.   I think that frog's legs are repulsive to eat.

3.   Jimmy went to the game to evaluate the opponent.

4.   Tammy is so shy and soft-spoken; Betsy likes to monopolize a talk.

5.   This faculty represents the best in the state.

6.   That long-winded man spoke in monotone.

7.   We must develop a plan to remodel our home.

8.   I like to read romantic novels.

9.   Mom cannot stand the mess that can accumulate in the shed.

10. Mr. Smith's explosive protest made Tommy erupt.

1. Let's stop here for rest and refreshments.

2. If that volcano explodes, it may be quite destructive.

3. We must get that equipment so that we can finish the job.

4. Ben had his trombone and Jake had his violin.

5. I must pass this math class to graduate.

6. I think the opponent has extensive help.

7. Jenny was impolite to her dad in the lobby of the hotel.

8. Itemize the bill and send them a copy.

9. Could Congress regulate the cost of gas?

10. We will help to promote the development of this product.

5.4

1. Jake represented Tom for the big case.

2. Pete rented a tuxedo to go to the prom.

3. Did Tom panic when he shot the elastic and it hit Mr. Cahill?

4. Hire a consultant to evaluate this program.

5. Jimmy will calculate the math problems before he goes to bed.

6. I hope that Betsy is open-minded when we discuss this problem.

7. The kids did not demolish the script.

8. We cannot isolate Tommy from the class.

9. A fantastic video club will open in the spring.

10. James thinks that Sally is too protective with her children.

1. The congressman would like to rejuvenate that old mill, but it would be too expensive.

2. Did the salesman discuss a novelty item?

3. Jake and Molly went out for espresso and hot, fresh, bran muffins.

4. Mr. Henry hopes to stimulate a state-wide program for the homeless.

5. James can assume the role of a diplomat.

6. The kids congregate at the donut shop.

7. Must we incubate these ostrich eggs?

8. A humanistic welfare program will help.

9. The state's economy is the best it has been in a long time.

10. The company's loss was reflective of a lack of sales.

5.4

Equipment Problem

A conflict became a problem at the Smith Company. It was about the use of equipment. The boss had neglected the problem until its development became explosive. He had to respond. At last, he had to regulate the use of the equipment. He did not wish to do this, but he felt it would combat the problem.

People had to complete a request for equipment time. This became an absolute requirement. People in the company were upset, but the boss insisted, and in the end, it did help with the conflict.

Jimmy and Betsy

Jimmy and Betsy did not have plans. They did not have company and so they were glad to just relax. Jimmy went to the video club and rented a romantic film for Betsy. They had plenty of junky refreshments.

Jimmy did not like the video film — he felt that it was silly. Betsy did not evaluate it so badly. She felt that it was O.K. Still, they did have a fun day. It felt good to just recline and be lazy.

The Explosive Volcano

been
now
people
their
lava

The siren blasted at nine a.m. All those native to the remote land had expected it. The destructive volcano had erupted. A plan had been made to evacuate and now there was no time left to prepare. People had to vacate their homes. Despite the plan, many did not wish to go, but they had to escape the hot, explosive lava.

Tommy Strum

The faculty at the Miltone High School was quite upset with Tommy Strum. He was defiant. He was impolite to the teachers and, at times, explosive. His disrespect made the teachers want to expel him.

Tommy did not care about the content of his classes. He did not fulfill the requirements. Most times he did not even attend.

Tommy did like to violate all the rules. He disrupted his classes, and the teachers felt they could not educate him until he committed himself to school. His mom and dad were insistent that he stop his delinquent way.

stigma	Donna	extra
comma	villa	antenna
umbrella	ultra	tundra
vodka	Edna	Atlanta
vista	delta	Anna

---

stanza	dogma	henna
Kenya	alfalfa	yucca
Calcutta	fibula	quota
scuba	gala	Emma
chinchilla	vendetta	vanilla

---

alive	awoke	abuse
adapt	amid	amaze
aloft	kabob	acute
anemic	amidst	pathetic
aside	abode	atone

Alaska	manila	arise
aline	adept	Apollo
abide	abandon	ability
abolish	agaze	amuse
atomic	manipulate	awaken

---

stabilize	stupidity	subsidize
subsidy	indirect	illuminate
fumigate	platinum	mutilate
scrutinize	optimistic	lubricate
manicure	halibut	subdivide

substitute	duplicate	instigate
silicone	implicate	sanitize
nominate	sensitive	optimum
mobilize	medicate	imitate
dominate	litigate	sentiment

divide	pimento	divine
altitude	antidote	difficult
cultivate	confident	estimate
complicate	indicate	dilute
Eskimo	institute	captivate

---

oxidize	illuminate	obligate
dignity	candidate	ventilate
fabricate	compliment	detriment
amplitude	entity	condiment
palpitate	culminate	pessimist

---

1. Donna must submit the script to Mr. Kimes.

2. Sally will complete the last stanza of her song.

3. Sandy will discuss the trip to Kenya at the club.

4. Tammy likes to add alfalfa to her salad.

5. Ed rented a French villa so that he could impress his gal.

6. Steve lost the antenna to his van in the crash.

7. The boss did not think we could make the sales quota, but we did.

8. Betsy did not bring her umbrella and now she regrets it!

9. The club will fly on a Delta jet to Atlanta.

10. Timmy insists that he will have extra time to visit his mom.

1. Edna will go take scuba lessons before she goes on her trip.

2. Anna has to get vanilla so she can make the cupcakes.

3. Sandra will invite Bob to the gala event.

4. Tim's instinct did amaze me.

5. Our company plans to abandon its attempt to compete in that product line.

6. We still cannot adapt to our new boss.

7. Pam plans to develop her ability in basketball.

8. The problem arose when the prospective sale did not happen.

9. With the conflict aside, Jim and Kate can begin the task.

10. If you come in late, take care not to awaken the children.

1. Despite the problem, the boss hopes to duplicate the sales.

2. We have had a substitute in class now for quite awhile.

3. Russel is confident in Ed's ability as boss in his company.

4. Mr. Banty is such an optimistic man, but his wife is so pessimistic.

5. Dave gave Sandra a compliment that made her blush.

6. The democratic candidate will visit this school.

7. If Tom takes time off now, it will complicate this mess even more!

8. I hope there is a way to ventilate the attic.

9. Beth's sensitive skin broke out in a rash.

10. Did Tommy nominate you for class president?

5.5

1. Glen plans to attend that institute and take up welding.

2. I can subtract fine, but I cannot divide well.

3. Did the baby try to imitate Jimmy?

4. It is difficult for Katy to ask for help; she is so shy.

5. The salesman will estimate the cost then give us a call.

6. Did the gals spend the cash for a manicure?

7. Lenny did not instigate the conflict.

8. Grandma must use an old antidote to save the puppy from the snake.

9. Did you indicate the problem when you spoke to him?

10. I think the only hope to get out of this mess is divine help!

A Sweet Treat

Donna went to the store to get some items. She did wish to make cupcakes. It would require vanilla, and she did not have this in the pantry.

When she came home, her husband was napping in the den. She made the cupcakes and frosted them. Then she went into the den to awaken her husband. When he awoke, he was glad to have a cupcake and milk. Donna got an extra kiss from him for her treat.

The Program Plan

Mr. Smith will reject the program plan. He will not adopt it until items are cut and some items are added. The basic plan fit his requirements, but he will insist his staff refine it. Mr. Smith will provide a profile that indicates his wishes.

Olympic
team
about
work
people
see

Golden Skates

Anna did hope to go to the Olympics for the U.S.A. She had spent so much of her life at the rink! She could skate well and was in tip-top shape. When Anna made the team, she had to prepare; she could not relax much. Anna was athletic and talented as well as intensive about her work. She had to be optimistic about her ability to win.

When Anna was a contestant in a contest, she was confident. She could captivate the people in the stands. Anna had plenty of fans that would respond to her difficult stunts. It was a thrill to see her skate.

The prospect of a gold medal gave Anna her drive. People predicted that she could possibly finish second, and she did compare with the top. Her best opponent was from Finland, and so much depended on the last event. A drastic mistake or even a small slip would effect the result.

Anna had one last skate and she could win the gold. She chose a song with a fast tempo. The fans began to clap as she began to glide across the ice. The fans in the arena sat in amazement when she did the difficult jumps. She was fantastic! The fans were explosive at the finish.

Anna did try her best for the gold. Her score did indicate that she could win. At last, the moment came. Anna had won the gold medal for the U.S.A.! Anna went to shake hands with the gal from Finland. Then she began to cry just a bit as she gave a big wave to the fans who were clapping wildly for her. The thrill was more than she had ever dreamed .

5.5

Post Test Step Five

she	mucus	fifty
communize	spry	tundra
rodent	sultry	skyline
awaken	Atlanta	amplitude
ruby	diagnosis	climax

---

stry	tridem	prespere
cre	po	gantly
blenet	nupe	shipe
rebect	flothine	ploton
scret	stomest	crozump
